GONE HAYWIRE AND OTHER OLD SAYINGS

Poems

by

William Zander

SERVING HOUSE BOOKS

Gone Haywire and Other Old Sayings

Copyright © 2010 William Zander

All rights reserved.

No part of this book may be used or reproduced in any manner whatsoever without the prior written permission of the copyright holder except for brief quotations in critical articles or reviews.

Cover and author photos by A.H. Zander

Thanks to George's Salvage Co., Newton, NJ, for the scene of the cover photo.

ISBN: 978-0-9825462-4-6

Serving House Books logo by Barry Lereng Wilmont

Published by Serving House Books
www.servinghousebooks.com

First Edition 2010

William Zander has published poetry in many periodicals (e.g., *Beloit Poetry Journal, Crazy Horse, Defined Providence, Light, New Letters, New York Quarterly, Nimrod, Poetry Northwest, Prairie Schooner, Rattapallax, South Dakota Review, Yankee,* et al.) and one book of poems, *Distances,* from Solo Press (long out of print). He is a contributing editor of *The Literary Review* and has retired from teaching at Fairleigh Dickinson University in Madison, New Jersey.

Acknowledgments

Some of these poems first appeared in various literary journals, and I wish to acknowledge them here. They are:

The Chattahoochee Review
Connecticut Review
Defined Providence
Light: A Quarterly of Light Verse
The Louisville Review
Naugahyde Literary Journal
New Letters
Nimrod International Journal of Prose and Poetry
Slant: A Journal of Poetry
South Dakota Review

Author's Note

All these poems come from a suite-in-progress I call *Old Sayings*. They are based on English clichés, bromides, idiomatic locutions, &c. Actually, "based on" is not correct; sometimes, a phrase is the starting point for a poem (e.g. "What Do You Want for Nothing?"), but at other times, a poem begins from the usual dark source and the title comes later.

The point is, this is a suite, not a sequence (like a sonnet sequence), so I feel free to use whatever starting point works, as well as whatever form or content works. So far, I've written everything from a prose poem to rime royal, from comic verse to rather heavy stuff, from poems with personal content to those with the impersonal emotion Eliot called for, lean poems and fat poems, bellowing poems and *sotto voce* poems.

The many phrases I've found, it seems to me, still have life, if heard from a certain angle; they represent the living language as it is now, powered by living breath. As titles, they seem to give a shape, a sort of verbal keystone, to all sorts of wacky and profound moods.

There are, I think, two meanings to the rubric *Old Sayings*. There is the one I originally intended (clichés &c.), and there is the fact that these poems are clearly in the voice of an increasingly old guy saying stuff.

—William Zander

Contents

I

11	Hymn: Plain as Day
12	He Wouldn't Hurt a Flea
13	No Rhyme or Reason
15	You've Got Another Think Coming
17	Leaving Little to Chance
19	It Doesn't Add Up
21	One Foot in the Grave
23	Facing the Music
25	Talking to Hear My Head Rattle
26	Stopped Dead in Your Tracks
28	Advice to the Lovelorn
29	What Do You Want for Nothing?
30	Famous Last Words
31	Lock, Stock, and Barrel
33	Getting Under His Skin
35	Beyond Belief

II

41	Gone Haywire

I

Hymn: Plain as Day

    Dawn fades in
when I least expect it.
Where are the books that held me once,
my brave invective,
the pictures forming in the darkroom?
    Memory leaves
with her usual lack of meaning,
a darkness with enormous breasts.
The facts open without
a message, as if it were a matter
of style. (In the place of death,
the nurse folds up the linen.)
    The constellations disappear,
quarks and quasars
lap at the edges. The universe
grows light, the mist in it
burns off, and I don't know
what emerges. Birdsong.
Something is buried here and it
will rise. Who knows? The angry
catbird wants me gone.

He Wouldn't Hurt a Flea

In the room
at the bottom of the stairs, the dank
basement with its fecal smells,
its dog hair, dustballs,
mountain of laundry,
helter-skelter distance
of lampshades, Christmas lights, old luggage,
cartons fat with fabrics,
unfinished knitting, sheet music,
letters, the rubble
of attics (if we had one) —
the keep, the barbican, the fortress
of fleas, the thought of fleas, the mad
obsession with fleas —
beside the dusty case of old
Americanas, mildewed LPs,
the boy, 13,
curled up on the floor,
reads to the dying dog
who will not eat, who can't stand up —
reads her books
by Dr. Seuss
("One Fish, Two Fish . . .").
The dog
is lying still
and seems to be listening
(". . . red fish, blue fish. . .").
In the confusion,
living and dead, that the house surrounds,
the fleas continue.

No Rhyme or Reason

1.
Gabe in one of those moods where he comes and goes
and disappears, upstairs, downstairs, over and over,
quiet, sudden, the lurker, the ghost
of the seventh grade.
                      Bright, sunny day,
windy, only a few wispy clouds
in the blue above the bright green banks
of trees.
          And for a moment I am not
in it.

        2.
        Trees rattling, gusty wind,
        he's in, he's out, he's
        somewhere.
        He appears in the kitchen:
        long head-banger's hair,
        white sweatshirt, loud Hawaiian shorts.
        School was OK? I ask him.
        Swings open the fridge
        and stares in.
        Gabe, don't just
        stand there with the door open.
        Huh? Oh, yeah.
        In the windows, close up,
            trees like green brains are in motion.

3.
The haunted windscape.
Nothing at all pinned down,
laundry and flags,

bricks and mortar,
kites without anyone to hold them.
The son
moving in and out
of the mind, the missing
link, the myth, the adolescent fear
of myself — and I almost smack
right into him
as I'm going out to the car.
Gabe!
Oh, sorry, Dad, I didn't see you.
Gabe,
is anything wrong? You seem jittery.
Trees swaying. Leaves fizzing.
No, no, it's OK.
Maybe something at school?
No — but Dad?
Yeah?
Do you know
if napalm will melt rubber?

    4.
    Everything
    so clear at last — each
    leaf where the wind
    shakes it. This
    is an erotic wind, and it
    will lift him.

You've Got Another Think Coming

— for Alex

No, no, hold it, I've had too much already,
Figure my tab, I'm finished, gotta go.
It's midnight. The ship's just easing past the jetty,
And I'm not Socrates, much less Rimbaud.
(When I was young, I thought the French were heady
And had *La Nausée* on my sloshed *bateau*.)
I'd like to drift like stardust on the deep.
But I've got miles to go before I leap.

Oh what the hell, Joe, set up another one,
Like — what is the final cause of being dead?
Why is there being at all instead of none?
Am I awake, like Gregor on his bed,
Or is there nothing new under the sun?
These questions hang like something made of lead,
An anchor going down — slowly, slowly.
I'll never plumb the depths! — or love you wholly,

Sweetheart. Joe, see what that lady's thinking.
Is she the Muse? My spouse? A feminist?
She seems to be staring at me, straight, unblinking,
Maybe enthralled with me, or maybe pissed.
What does it mean, this linking and unlinking
Across great distance? Does she even exist?
(Now there's a think that's been around so long
It's like a golden-oldie jukebox song.)

She gives me fever. So give me penicillin.
Joe, I've been through the mill, from the pre-Socratic
Dam builders to Wittgenstein and Dylan.
I've even ruminated on ecstatic
Links with God, but like some Blakean villain,
Mork or whoever, forged a world so static,
That nothing lived in it. Except, alas,
For me. I longed for sacraments. For mass.

Another thaw. The icy water stuns
The nerves of my hand, pauses, plunges through
The spillway to the pond where mayfly duns
Blink open on the surface, just a few —
Little things, little things, bear scat, axions,
Wood ducks or wood frogs quacking in the slough,
A reddish vapor over the maple limbs,
The viruses of childhood, and its hymns.

What does *what* mean? It means I'm dry, Joe,
Dry as the land surrounding the Euphrates
With all its endless warfare. That being so,
Bring me and the lovely — whoops, I see the lady's
Gone. Yet I remember her: the glow
Of her eyes, like someone just come up from Hades,
Who saw me with my mind tied up in knots
And loved me till I had no other thoughts.

Leaving Little to Chance

Everything cooking, everything going,
a juggling act, a balance between
nothing and burning, something or other
keeping it going, always in motion,
chopping, splitting, blending,
doing, undoing, whisks and spoons
rattling like crazy, spatulas
scraping, everything cooking,
eggs and bacon, burgers and fries,
corned beef and cabbage, pasta
al dente, broiled bluefish,
brains à la York, brioches, butterscotch,
chicken timbales, cucumber soup,
cauldrons simmering, steaming,
everything cooking, someone or other
leaving nothing alone, rushing
from cupboard to counter to stove,
making sure that everything's cooking,
even the coffee perking for later,
for leisure, the vigil lights of the burners
glowing, everything cooking,
loaf cakes, layer cakes, pound cakes,
Yorkshire pudding, quiche Lorraine,
blanquette de veau, coquilles St. Jacques
Derridá, duxelles, halibut, hare
(hash for tomorrow), peas and carrots,
garbanzos and peppers, pineapple popcorn,
porcupine, mei goo gai pen,
everything cooking, everything sizzling,
all systems go, adrenalin,
pistons, turbines, Mount

St. Helens, someone or other
forgetting the potholder, cursing
the wondrous idea that everything's cooking,
ragout and rarebit, rhubarb and rice,
Brunswick stew, shellfish and Sauternes,
soufflé and silence, spinach and squash,
turtles and tongue, biscuit tortoni,
pilaf, fritters, gnocchi,
everything cooking, something lost
in commotion, something falling apart
like an old cobweb, something or other
unavailable for sweet
or terrible surprises —
the riddle of the Märchen,
the book of hours, bloodlight, even
those wallowings, those sobs
in a single place, those mysteries
of doing nothing.

It Doesn't Add Up

How paltry life seems: mine, yours,
The mailman's, hapless agitated dross
Dividing, filling wombs and sewers,
Nailed and wriggling on a cross,

Sprayed as a pest at country clubs,
Flapping, drowning, standing tall,
Marching to Popes or Beelzebubs,
Flipped on a grill, gunned down at a mall —

So what's the choice? Eat or be eaten.
The earth itself is a rich stew,
A hot cauldron to toss the meat in.
Meaning, the mailman. Me. You.

As if inclined to slash their wrists,
Many have brooded thus, including
(*Ubi sunt?*) the Modernists.
It's paltry, too, all this brooding.

My favorite Modernist is Hardy.
He knew what "hap" meant. Also "twain"
Converging, as when, doing 40,
Making a poem in my brain

(This one, as it happens), giving
Little heed to nature, I catch,
From my eye's corner, something living
Dart from the woods and into the path

Of my car — "Damn it!" — and disappear.
I swerve, slam on the brakes, stall,
Get out and hurry back to where
It may not have happened, a green wall:

But there it lies on the asphalt, furry,
Soft and limp like a child's beanbag,
A chipmunk, no longer in a hurry,
A chance occurrence without meaning,

Only a dot of red on its snout
To show that this is meat to please
An avid crow. Meanwhile, my route
Proceeds, between the walls of trees.

How paltry life seems, yours, mine,
This poem's, if it has any,
The snap and crackle of every line
Seeming to fizzle out, like static.

A poem *doesn't* live, not really.
It has no eyes, no spine, no liver.
What you suppose is a poem's feeling
Isn't, though it last forever.

Feelings don't. I think of my father,
Clutching my hand, a paltry thing
Like a chipmunk, a feeling, just another
Death. So. Why this lingering?

One Foot in the Grave

Mehr Licht! Mehr Licht!

Dragging it around
like a bear trap,
limping with an ugly,
unpredictable lurch
like the club-footed
heir apparent,
I am still
a creature in the world.

Sometimes, driving home
at night, maybe after
a couple of beers,
free at last of the earth's
pull, my car immense
with Bach, I am
deep, like a well
that plumbs the universe.

Daylight, glaring,
gets thick again with work.
I swear, caught up in it,
snagged by a million
tiny snares like some
poor soul in a masterpiece
by Bosch, all my struggles
making things worse,

or like a B movie
villain, sinking
in what I thought was solid
ground: the years.
Only my hand
is up as if I had
a question. And the living
light above me blurs.

Facing the Music

— for Alex

It starts like a whisper in your head,
Or a low humming, distant hooting,
A Barred owl, chorus frogs in March,
A dark horizon line of pines
Where a tune is hovering in the air,
Simple, available, that fills
     Your being, then more of you,
Flowing like water through a fish's gills.

Then it begins to throb, to swell,
To form itself in lines and layers,
Woodwinds, brass, continuo,
The choir in complex harmony,
Cantatas, masses, simple prayers
A holy challenge! And so you keep
     To the stepping stones of Bach,
A way over the water, which is deep.

And it swells some more, cracking, uncoiling,
Opening to the abyss of self;
The strings intensify, the horns
Announce the engulfing wave of Frühling:
Mahler's languid sprawl, tumescent
Neuroses — nostalgia for the past,
     Spring flowers, children, the voice
That rang so pure for God, that didn't last.

Sad, sad. And finally, irritating,
A nagging, techno throb, not even
The steady tomtom of desire,
More like a jingle on TV
Drilling you to be a buyer
Of gum, cosmetics, beer that's made
    From Rocky Mountain water.
So you stand in line, weary, if unafraid.

Still, the sadness stays, a long
Liturgical chant, the vigil lights
Flickering on the stove at midnight,
Staccato of coughing from the bedroom,
Drained blue arteries of trees
In the kitchen windows. Here where you putter,
    Water steams away
From the kettle. The house is thick with cold, dark matter.

Facing the music must be like —
Rethinking your life perhaps? (Breaking
The old, shellac records over
Your husband's head!) The music's under
A trapdoor, swollen shut. (The husband
Walks in water, casting a fly,
    Finding it hard to believe
That a whole ocean could at last go dry.)

Talking to Hear My Head Rattle

As if something inside is loose,
a belt, a bearing, a dozen bolts,
a couple of million brain cells —
what if someone profound, like God
or Miss Scolla in the fourth grade,
were listening to this racket?

Who cares, when nothing's working?
I think it means I'm giving up the ghost,
something making me jittery,
something suddenly shooting up my spine
like a chimney fire — something about
childhood, the prison that never knew me.

Maybe it's notes from underground,
drills probing the mine, the noise of the earth-shaker,
the rumbling, the preparation, the new me
about to erupt — and maybe not,
maybe it's just my Muse with her maracas,
her tall hat full of bananas.

Something, I say, is loose,
something truer than art — yes! — the blown gasket
between the brain's two halves,
the clean connection that should let me sing
the Song of Myself
so the world out there can understand it.

Stopped Dead in Your Tracks

— for Adlai

It stopped you at dusk: the deer's head —
on a heap of limbs and guts, cored ribcage that had held
its heartbeat — staring! lifelike!
left where anyone could stumble over it
as you did, along the road bordering the fish-and-game land,
simply dumped, like old tires —
except that head, upright, carefully placed,
a joke, like "Here's the Head," mounted over the john at some
two-bit roadhouse.
                      You picked it up
and held it like the skull of Yorick:
mouth that has forsaken browsing,
brain that has forsaken dreaming,
eyes that have forsaken — no, it seemed to you those eyes,
those famous, lovely eyes, were still alert,
still had depth — and something in me said,
How trite, Bambi with the big brown eyes, the bad
men in their flame-fluorescent coats.

    But then, you aren't naive, you've seen plenty
of dead deer, wouldn't have been shocked
to come upon it in the woods — but to have it dumped
along the road! the scarecrow head! It wasn't fitting,
it wasn't seemly. (You shook, you wept
when you told us, the teen-age wise guy
swallowed up.) You said that holding it was like
holding your dog's head — just so, I see it, I feel it,
the head you patted and scratched behind the ears,
the brisk fur, the soft ears. Adlai! I don't blame you,
give up meat, give up your own shameful

humanity. But remember this:
When you find your woman and hold her like the source of life,
think of entrails, think of the inside of the body.
Think of yourself, the severed self:
It seems to be deep, doesn't it? Like the deer's eyes.
　　You carried the head from the roadside into the woods,
the darkness, a semi-sacred place
(you must have stumbled). Adlai, my head bursts
with lessons for you, wagging their tails like a pack of hounds!
(They take off after the fox.
You like to see him leave them in the lurch.)

Advice to the Lovelorn

Nothing's as wonderful as having sex.
Hopefully, you have it. There's nothing to it.
And having nothing can make us nervous wrecks,
So my advice is, don't just have it, do it.
Actually, it's now or never. What
Do you want for nothing? Someone who will mean it,
Scheme it, ream it? Come on, get off your butt!
Someone will want it, maybe, if you clean it.
You're feeling kinda blue, huh? No wonder!
The thermonuclear sun is running faster,
God's in His heaven, you'll be x feet under.
But a dog in heat's a dog, whoever its master.
Better than being nothing. Better than
Being some burnt-out meaning, like, Man.

What Do You Want for Nothing?

Something, a pill, a shot, an overdose,
The Truth, the Song of Songs, the soup du jour,
Something spiritual or something gross,
A whore, a sacrament, a catheter,
Whatever physic will effect a cure,
A salve, an ointment, an emollient
To soften my thick skull, my heart of flint —

Something to ease the soul (a draught of vintage?),
Something to clear my inner being (bran?),
Something to give me strength (a can of spinach?),
Something worth dying for (the Rights of Man?) —
My life's a mess! I need a moving van
To cart it off, but first an EKG,
Doctor, to find my heart in the debris.

O take me to a place where I can stop
Biting myself for God, the open wound,
To the 1940s starring Mom and Pop,
A soldier and his girl who sat and spooned
While on the radio a singer crooned
"You Are Always in My Heart," the future grim
But full of faith that she would wait for him.

I'm waiting for advice from the Dalai Lama
A clue a crutch a piece of cake a creed
A beast a bubble a carrot stick a comma,
Silence, a new P.C., a mustard seed,
A resounding line of poetry. I need
Transfusions, CPR, a transplant, art,
Something to get it up (I mean my heart).

Famous Last Words

Time to go, be done, like a frozen lake
Becoming slush in August, like a shelf
Of *National Geographics*, like a fruitcake,
Like LPs, like playing with oneself.
Time to present the ultimate one-liner,
To whisper my confession to the priest,
To sink into corruption and decline
Like the Roman empire — to be, at last, a beast,
Food for worms, and hold the literature!
Time to cut out the idle, empty talk,
The daily lack of meaning and its jury.
Time to catch a thermal like a hawk
At the equinox. Time to be on my way.
Time to screech whatever I have to say.

Lock, Stock, and Barrel

All gone, goodbye, my hoards of stuff
Turned into froth and foam. Farewell,
Lumpy appurtenances, fluff,
Bongos, books, the Liberty Bell
Untolling. Like a dump, I smell.
Like you, I've had enough.

I'm chucking it all, putting a finger
Down my throat (in a pig's eye,
Says Mort, the stark and devious bringer
Of false hope and humble pie).
Even the phone off the hook's a lie,
A myth, a humdinger,

Like the one that God counts up the hairs
That sprout from my head (are they so dear?),
Or the big one, that He even cares.
I want it shaven, Zen-like, clear,
An empty vessel that will hear,
But will not say, its prayers.

Meanwhile, my little forklift scurries
From place to place with crates of thought
I want to unload. Like the furies,
They buzz and beep, and all for naught.
I'm longing for an unzoned spot
Where only the river hurries,

The river, an archetype, slack
Or intense, pell-mell or sinuous,
A source, a plunge, amnesiac
Of hung-up tackle, trailers, dross
Of flesh that turns anonymous.
The river. It won't be back.

Getting Under His Skin

"Whoa — is that a snake back there?" I ask my son. I brake
and back up cautiously. The curled, black,
three-dimensional shape in the mirror — it *could* be
a tire tread, I hope, but no, I see already two
pink splotches where its guts have popped
out of its skin — a small black rat snake
on the sparkling asphalt, deep in the suburbs,
culture of power tools and neighbors like ourselves:
Who could have done this in the dense, autumn sunlight?
But now, looking down from the window, I see it's not
dead, the sharp tail is twitching, the head is slightly raised
like Lawrence's snake in Italy. My son gets out.
"We ought to finish him off," I say. "See any rocks?"
He looks around him. Shrubs and driveways,
Andersen windows staring blankly out at us,
shards of leaves starting to fill the lawns.
The boy, with his cropped hair, his black flight jacket,
looks down at the snake through a kind of numbness.
And the snake, its head raised in a graceful arc,
seems to be looking back, gently, steadily,
as if it understands what he is feeling,
his agitation, his bleakness.
At last my son looks up at me, framed in the open
driver's window. "Can we just run over him?" he asks.
I am befuddled by sunlight, bad nerves and too many
appointments with therapists and students. And anyway,
a couple of cars appear over the rise,
coming toward us in the other lane,
the lane where the snake lies dying in its skin that looks like

carbon steel — too late, too late.
"Come on," I say, "we'll be late."
And he does, and we don't look back as the gleaming cars pass by, going the other way.

Beyond Belief

There is a town in the desert without flags,
Without signs, without even graffiti,
Without lights except for constellations
To show you where you are, "middle of nowhere,"
As they say, those quaint geographers
Who once assured you there was nothing there.
But you knew better, even then. You knew
That shimmering mirage on the horizon
Was something burning.
                           All night long, the wind
Howls down from the mountain passes, driving dust
That fills the air, blurring moon and stars,
Finding the cracks in so-called solid stuff
Until it settles, somewhere, anywhere,
Like you — if only *you* could be lifted!
                                          Briefly
It stops, day dawns petrified, the eastern
Sky turns gunmetal gray, the mountains a kind of
Sickly pink. Slowly the photograph
Develops, the wreckage of the town rises,
A warm breath touches your face, the world
Speeds up, something metallic flaps and bangs,
Tumbleweeds go rolling through the streets
Like human heads, pieces of paper fly.
   A railroad track injects itself into
The town and out, as if afraid,
Furtive. Whatever's left is boarded up,
Shut down. (You once believed that everyone
Was his own lake. And you thought there must be ways
Out of the water.)

           Beyond belief, at the rim,
A faded, bubble-headed gas pump stands
Surveying things, like an alien from a saucer:
Blackened, hollow car bodies and trailers,
Buildings with their roofs caved in, charred
Studs and shingles, a froth of smells, burnt
Rubber, plastic, horsehair furniture-stuffing,
Creosote, bile, grease, a fifty-five-
Gallon drum that still holds something dreadful.
You know this place: it's all those years of seeking
The self in its gilded frame.
                        Surely, you say,
something else exists beyond belief,
No one thinks that this is the way things are,
Everyone knows there's "real life," even here,
Like — who knows? — beyond that rock, a sidewinder
Unwinding, sand-colored, seeking body heat,
Like yours.
             A hummock of tires looms over
The scattered TV sets with bashed-in tubes,
Defunct appliances, rusty cans, shards
Of vinyl records, bedsprings, bones, a clock,
A woman's slip that floats by in the wind,
The dust, the flying scraps of paper, pages
From calendars and comics, tacky novels,
Literary stuff (*Perspective*, *kayak*),
Forgotten letters, someone's stamp collection
Freed, unhinged, whirling about, bits of
Rhodesia, *Deutsches Reich*, United States —
Words! Who could make choices here? The wind
Plays itself, over and over, like a jukebox
Honky-tonking the same, obsessive tune,
Someone's reminder, someone's sense of loss.

    Beyond belief is you, yes, the middle
Of nowhere, almost at home there, too, as if
You had built it, though you can't help looking back
To the place you longed to leave.
                                    Beyond belief
There is a roaring torrent. It is what is,
Your life, the dream of water going elsewhere.

II

Gone Haywire

— for Gabe

> ... the Lord of hosts has a day against all that is proud and lofty, against all that is lifted up and high, against all the cedars of Lebanon, lofty and lifted up; and against all the oaks of Bashan; against all the high mountains, and against all the lofty hills; against every high tower, and against every fortified wall. ...
>
> —Isaiah 2:12-15
>
> ... young men must live.
>
> —Falstaff, in 1 Henry IV, 2.2

1.
His revelation: whatever blood-light the Lord
demanded of my son that night,
it came out ragged, full of holes, the message
mangled like road kill. He was beyond
fear, flapping like his totem eagle over
the dark streets.
        Held down
on the gurney by the cops, he was read
the fact of the needle, and he
curled up like a child
and fell asleep.

2.
A satori, as he called it, had awakened
him from fear.
He had stayed locked in for days
with the handwriting on the wall (his own
tormented graffiti),
his high-rise apartment totally trashed,
moldy dishes, broken
refrigerator, clothes and spilled containers
strewn on the floor.
                    Meanwhile,
someone was right outside
in the hallway, smoking,
now and then
slipping pieces of paper
under the door.

3.
His satori also opened for him
a prodigious vision:
the Great Millennial Flood brought on by global warming,
the last survivors clinging to
the immense antennae on the World Trade Center towers,
great white sharks circling in their element,
picking people off
as the heaving waters rose even higher.

4.
This was before the summer of the sharks,
the turning of the Twin Towers into
ashes and dust,
in the first year of the honest-to-God
millennium, 2001,
reams of paper flying out
against the black smoke.

5.
My son, my son! his voice ranting
in the wilderness of Newark in the warm
(global warming!) winter of 1999,
stalking the streets, pigeon-holing
panhandlers and crackheads, proclaiming
the baptism of fire and the sword
when all they wanted was bread, man,
bread. "We are all native Americans!"
he shouted, grabbing them by their
hands, their arms, or even (in my case)
the shirt collar,
twisting it in a way that was
foreign, as if I were a prisoner of war.
"Shut up!
Shut up! You always tell me
I don't listen!"

6.
Two years before
the summer of the sharks, the fall
of the Temple of Mammon, the Great Satan,
container for the thing contained,
hearts, bones,
incessant flesh that struggled to get out,
container for the thing contained.

7.
Tower of Babel, Twin Towers,
transcendent latticework
of glass and steel, sinking,
sunk. Eerie, like trying to imagine
a black hole.

8. *A survivor*
"Can you see sky?"

9.
The summer of the shark,
2001—how paltry
this seems now! The uncle
pulling his nephew's arm
from the bull shark's gullet, a mere
curiosity among so many body parts.
Nature's revenge,
my son predicted.
Light a votive candle for them.

10. *The son*
"I had the bandana around my neck
and my face all smudged with black like a
working-class terrorist. I saw
on the street that everyone
was wearing a bandana; girls
would be wearing white, while guys
were wearing red—yuppies, homies,
whoever. I'd seen all these people
before. I'd forgotten. And then
the phone rang in a booth I just
happened to be passing, and sure
enough, when I picked up the receiver,
it was dead.
            "How did you
do it, Dad? How did you
set me up for that one?"

11.
A system
crashes. The so-called
facts—financial reports,
Powerpoint printouts, airline receipts,
telephone bills, employee manuals—
strewn on the ashen streets and sidewalks.

12.
Tower of Babel,
Twin Towers,
information highway
zooming skyward—
"Forgive!" he said.
"Love me!" she said.
The road went up, up and away
into the blue, away
from the flame and smoke. And they
grasped each other's hand
and jumped.

13. *The son*
"I'd been walking around all day.
What happened was, people on the street
kept giving me clues on where to go.
All this is some kind of experiment.
I have an instinct that says Ronnie had
something to do with it. You know
how my mind was all jumbled up?
You thought I had A.D.D., which, I've figured out,
is just some Western trait—anyway,
now my mind is in perfect order."

14.
Tower of Babel, Twin Towers—
the mind can't stand to be everywhere!
Polyglot chaos, dispersal of voices,
tongues of flame, raw sound
like a jet diving.

15.
Ladies and gentlemen,
This is your captain speaking.
It is time to say your prayers.

16.
The tight-lipped spoor of desire,
labels, trade names,
papers and diskettes crammed at the last minute
into a briefcase.
And they all converge, these people who had been
virtual in their cubicles,
and jam the exits. Down they go
and around, down and
around the endless
stairway. "Excuse me."
Making jokes
as the steel buckles.

17.
Swept away,
words in megabytes and flickering pixels,
ghostly paper blown in the firestorm,
banks of data
from which we had tried to fish, while overhead
a lone helicopter without a clue
is flying from tower to tower.

18. *A survivor*
"We could see things twisting
and flipping in the sunlight,
pieces of metal and glass,
and it suddenly dawned on us:
that stuff is coming after us!"

19. *A survivor*
"This thing jumped me! It had enough force
to lift me right out of the water. It felt like
a truck had slammed into me. Then I felt
a compacting squeeze,
an acute burning in my leg."

20.
Skeletal lattice looming behind them,
the great cranes and grapplers lurch over
the smoking debris, poking through
the gobbledegook of steel,
concrete slabs bristling with rebar,
shards of glass, pulverized Sheetrock,
tangled skeins of red cable—
as if death were a great
Dumpster.
          Count!
Count them. How many body bags
will not be needed?

21. *A survivor*
"We all washed out our
mouths. You'd be amazed
at what came out, at what was
plugged up our noses and ears and in
the backs of our throats."

22.
The "wacko ward," as he calls it,
nurses, orderlies,
the feeling of being in
a submarine. We bring him
a "Care package" from Burger King,
find our niche in the cramped
visitors' room. He's cranky,
irritable, wants out, but even more,
a cigarette. "Come on,
smuggle some in for me, will you?"
His t-shirt says "The Casualties,"
the name of a punk band.
He paces, swears, cracks
his knuckles. No more visions,
no satori, now he's just
one of the gray people, all burnt out,
a shade to bring gifts to.

23.
Blahblahblah.
The dead don't mutter.
The dead don't dance in the mosh pit
and play loud music.
The dead don't fuss and fart
and rant in the streets
or in my house. And of course:
"... none do there, I think, embrace."
(The irony waves bye-bye
and jumps, like Berryman,
but doesn't die like him. Oh no!)
Let me make one thing
perfectly clear:
This was supposed to be a poem

about a sick young man
living on his own in a "blighted city"
where he had what's called a "nervous breakdown."
(Words elude me.)
His prodigious vision was right out of an artless
disaster film.
No historical value here,
no event.
Maybe my heart imploded, that's all.
Maybe I'm heartless.

24.
Terror and pity.
I'm not the Tin Man, no,
more like Batman, high above
Gotham, brooding over
Ground Zero.
Unreal city! Unreal city!

25.
"I don't need this," my son says
through his teeth. "I don't need this. I can't
find my fucking cap." And I can feel the knot
tighten. He paces, picks up magazines, hymn books,
starts flinging the stuff about. What next?
Fist through the wallboard? A window?
"Son, wait," I say. "Fuck you,
old man. You wuss. You sorry
piece of shit." Later, he comes back
weeping, hugging me, begging
forgiveness. "I can't live like this,"
my wife says. I turn cold,
delete myself. I can't live. I can't
live, say the whole outdoors, the frozen

constellations. The dog
jars me, yanks on her leash
to poke her nose in the roadside leafpile,
sniffing for the perfect place to pee.

www.ingramcontent.com/pod-product-compliance
Lightning Source LLC
Chambersburg PA
CBHW031436040426
42444CB00006B/832